LOCAL WOMAN

Jzl Jmz

LOCAL WOMAN

Nightboat Books
New York

Printed in the United States

ISBN: 978-1-643-62273-6

Design and composition by Kit Schluter
Typeset in Perpetua and **Neue Kabel**

Cover photograph by Efraín Mojica

Cataloging-in-publication data is available
from the Library of Congress

Nightboat Books
New York
www.nightboat.org

“Give you all the depths of my wanting
Stays to for the rest of the morning
Give you the world that you seem to know
Yeah, I’ma get it”

"Jerrod" x When I Get Home (2019) x Solange

“Love you, then they switching They be huntin’, I’m bewitching
Get these bitches in they ’maginary, temporary feelings
Mutha what you do to these bitches
I be exisiting”

"Ovulate" x bbymutha

Contents

LOCAL WOMAN

Local Woman Does Woman Things

She bleeds & gets called beautiful by men.
  luxuriates the wonder of womanhood.
  curves in new ways with each lunar phase.

She births language in the mirror's gaze.
  knows violence as a lover.
  finds a way to form a fist with gel-x nails.

My body does forgiving things. She does laborious things.
  grieves what gestates loss. sees the gaps in her pay.
  sees who is missing & murdered beside her.

She is the fantasy in someone else's head. She is my choice.
She is my vessel down any available avenue.
She has a history of harrowing hikes home.

My body was born in the shadow of a man.
  produces significant levels of estrogen.
  drips fish. fears current infection.

She takes preemptive care.
  so she can open herself freely again.
She tells her girlfriends how tender her breasts are becoming.

My body receives, enthusiastically.
She claims penetration as pinnacle.
She is a hole. She is used. She dodges danger daily.

She does become a tool. She wrenches herself.
    around vice without vexation. My body romances.
She cannot currently cultivate her lush in the liminal.

My body does
what She needs
& names it necessary.

Local Woman Is Only Devoted to One Messiah

For Grindr

Myself, but I tarry here for his late-night revival.

White Jesus of Portland climbed down off a Tennessee cross,
rose from a cold-brew communion with carpenter's shoulders
& what he emphasizes as an OPEN relationship.

I prey on his weeping endurance before morning joy.

He, a beer-soaked savior of loose wall sockets
& unfinished shelves, was looking for rest in my weary land.
He confesses every thought out of sync & ignorant of sin.

I decide he can wash my feet, he can attempt a miracle.

He rises again & again & I laugh at his retrograde.
He leaves me unraptured but redeemed for a second time.
He isn't the first to say he needs my laying-on-of-hands.

Obligation #22 (TRANSLUCENCE)

I am the reflection of something that is.
I lit this fantasy myself. I need you too.
See it like I do, at least once. Don't lie to me.

I know flimsy when I write it. Ethereal.
Epidermis. An edict on everything.

That evaporates. Skin of unshowable debt.
Face of featured fabrication. Full-time fixture.

Think of how long light takes to travel across space.
All we recognize is the varied diffusion.
The slight slice of spectrum. We call our vision.
Naked. Despite density, we appear as films.
Screens, scrims, stages, veins, & crosses
  seen through luxe light.

Imagine the appearance of a thing but not.
The Thing itself. This is how we are taught to love.
What can be projected from imagination?
A truth will travel slower than the speed of light.

Space is more expansive than I'd ever be.
I am the reflection of something that is.

Drenched in Reflection

Cause we're not allowed in public, not really.
My mom thinks everyone is enamored with my beauty,
But I know they are surprised to see one of us
Living. Outside is a stage & I'm a pretty player.
I love what I see on the other side of myself.
A man tells my mother he couldn't take the doll,
Because my heels, my legs, my tattoos stopped
Him from looking me in the eye. He wants to meet
Me, to apologize for eating me from my sole up.
He's the worst I'm aware of, but not alone in lust-
Filled gaze givers. All I want to tell my mother
About me. How they like my parts. She thinks
I'm unclockable until I speak & I know she's trying
Not to blame me for any danger I dodge. Desire
Is in the eye of the beholder, but I live in the empty
Hands of discombobulated bastards. Disintegrate
In their salivating. I am shards of selves
They wish to suck between their teeth.

Local Woman Raises Lazarus

After Sylvia Plath

I have wanted again
each day a walking miracle, my skin
soft as a weekly needle,

My waistline, a paperweight
my face a shifting, queen-
size pillowcase

Untuck the dripping
my paramour
do I satisfy?

The supple, tightness, the full use of hands?
The sour throat
will last only

Then, then my flesh
A grave dug, ate out
my home in me

& like the cunt, I have no time to lie
Sir.
These are my hands
My tongue
I may be rare and willing

Irregardless, I am the same woman you wanted
Dying
is a poem, I can finish myself
I do it exceptionally well

I do it so it feels like rent
I do it so it feels lasting
Which is to say

Fuck, I'm beautiful
I'm my own knockout
I never charge

For the eyeing of my thirst, I never charge
For the playing of my role
I'm really something
& I never charge, enough, at least
for my word or touch
or bits of blood

Then, Mr. Paramour
I am yours, open
I am yours, presently
The secret silver medal

I'll melt to a shriek
I moan and groan
Only you underestimate your great concern

Drip, drip—
I toss and gaze
Sweat, spit, there is nothing real

Mr. Daddy, Mr. BabyBoy
You close?
You close.

Footsteps in the Dark to the Edge of Objectivity pts. 1&2

I've been avoiding
elsewhere distractions
The tissue pillowing
on my chest
filling my grasping moments
having a body
for what had you
Want residing
in me
with no mercy
There is
an uncertainty principle
holding up the refrain
I can
now more than ever
I may have
resolved
to be my own
balladeer
Each beat
a consideration
A memory. It was

this time
of now, thin
haunted
by local men
& their dogs
Fiend
for any
conveniently
sourced strange
My romantic nature
at the genetic level
My new chemistry
can't stop
cascade-lyric
falling from interior cliffs.
My mind
drifting
now & then
between concordant &
dystopian
but in every future
I'm in love

Local Woman Implies Surplus

For M.Y.

Rawhide Father & I met
in a canyon of beets
& meat-packed moccasins.

Annexed to a syrup-city
where the hometown heroes
spoke in a collective we.

Outside of few friends,
mostly visitors themselves,
I found the settlers most allergic
to alarms & practicality of hushed tones.

Secrets of entitled dust
settled in the corner
of each townsperson's mouth.

He was passing through
fluent in railroad tracks
& impoverished steel.
He translated tumbled weed
from each torch-taught millennial mobster.

It was the first time I ventured
to terrain this unfamiliar
in the middle of a perpetually lost country.

He made me wonder
how many dead-ends exist within me.
We left the cause-&-effected canyon
together. We exhaled our sweet potato throats in tandem.
Rawhide Father returned
to what was left of his desert home.
He lanterned himself into holidays & houseshows.

We corresponded cartoons & favorite words
on any wind that could carry our refrains.

He talked to me like I was an endless highway.
I can always almost feel a breeze in his tone.

Even when it sounds like a frustrated downpour,
his voice is the flit of a shower.

When a fire breaks out in the desert,
he began to ash himself into every chord
he knows how to strum.

He made a candlewick chorus
to mourn the aftermath of heat.

I raindropped lyrics of humorous tomorrow
& open-handed compliments. I saw the brush
blazing from the hills. I smelled the smoke
from my whole world away.

I am only so much lumber.
I never want to imply surplus,
only combustibility.

By the time he simmers,
I engulfed his letters in yesterday.
My verse isn't his song
& the blood in the face is only his.

Yet, like all fires,
he is only extinguishable in this state.
I shed my predisposition to living in soot.

Obligation #21 (TRANSPARENCY)

In the mirror   she appears as
         I graze her stomach   this angle
faith is enough   glass barrier

between maybe   material &
         most of me can be happy
being cellophane sex siren

I lust for open-source lovers

all my underneaths   light exposed
         reflected back to me through
illusion   not ev'ry mirror
         is a parallel dimension

sometimes the otherside just is

Local Woman Acts Much Too Alone in Her Body, Yet Lonely No More

After Rainer Maria Rilke

She tries to maximize her hours
She believes too small in this world, yet smaller
  she dreams
to be an easy objective thing:
Black and svelte.
She says her best self needs accompanying.
The flight which lands to perform
& questions "who knows the way to the corner?"
where she can observe what is up.
She is among those who want to know
or else she be left alone.

I want to mirror her image to your tenderest seduction,
only *play* shy or undeserving.
Maintain the length of her long lingering gaze.
I want to refract her
Everywhere. The lush I dream is still latent.
I am dishonest to say she doesn't want more.
I want her reflection to be
Everything. Before you,
she calls herself a muse, a pin-up from heaven,
a fixture, a fantasy, fungible & finite
like a new material that upcycles naturally,
like the crow's bagel,
like my mother's genius,
like a satellite singing symphonies
from every frequency of free.

The HRT

After Pablo Neruda

I have hurt. You, my body,
I have starved your gut.

Misunderstood weight.
No one knows how I am,
but that "I am so much."
New chemical insides
for you.

In you I measure, wait
& lie awake unpatient.
You like all beings
demand
to see me reactive
& your ache
of acrylic & mirror
must form my chest
when she settles for the night.

Here's how I name you a firm stone.
Soft hands caress over your skin
oiling your expanses
& the soft that I want,
& if I feed
only your immaterial hunger, if I fill
nothing. What supports the dramatic
devastating form, confront

my weakness & my impulse,
my manicured hands
poisoning you a bit
so that you may exhale from
the fashioning of my terrors.

Demonstration Means Estradiol

For Bubba

Drawing 0.5 mL of clairion fluid from the vial to the vein
becomes an act of vanity simply because the commitment
to regulate pain provides such gains. The nurse likened my
[demonstration] to syrup, I instinctively likened it to lube.
She agreed but I was still embarrassed. I'm a different woman
now. I could have enjoyed that vulgarity beneath my surface.

I'll take my fifth dose of [demonstration] on the next full moon in Pisces.
I joke to Summer Boyfriend about being a fish whenever we eat salmon or cod.
Each dose gets me closer to new deltas. Every river tributaries
to greater waterways. My womanhood terraforms my chest
on either side of the stream & each of my lovers already has laid claim.
As of late, I've demanded even more gentleness
& each of my lovers recognizes
& reminds me of my conditional nature.

Titania Sings Mariah Carey at Midsummer Karaoke

I'm cursed with common rate nightmares of donkey-headed dreamboats
I blame my own magic's jealousy but I'd risk my life to feel

a humorous groundling on my pressèd flowers in my sleepless solitude
I sweat in the wintertime like a midsummer fever over hill, over dale

overwhelmed wildfire window is open year-round in the memory
of a song wake to purge mortal grossness vividly emblazoned in my mind

imagine my waxen thighs my un-right heart, am I not your distant star
wish? gentle mechanics to mine ear, mine eye till thy force doth move me

cause I'm drowned in you & I can't pull through the jeweled deep
knowing all this wet ain't just tears, what to do with moonbeams?

have I not stolen enough honey-bags from humble-bees to not be lonely?
to have My All to bed & to arise: plucked & painted butterfly.

Presently, I Only Want to Understand Being Full & Feeding

a Fever I'm trying to break reminds me to take in the Half-moon.
Chronic oscillation of Light & opacity. the Crescent cannot cure
Sickness. tide works keeping all the Raucousfolk limber branches.
Howling. a Jumpbrush howl. Just beneath jaw swelling. Lymphnode
lipsync. Mouthstuff is actually all I need to feel better. redirect
unkissed lips into proper applications into temporary leg paralysis
& free electrical rewiring. a light. Lighter to flick. Scratcher to itch.
my Nails in better care than my Stomach. keep a Roof, kept
in Grace. hunger begets need begets rocket launches to Places
post-why & Probably still pre-knowledge. ancient mathematics
have become dietary Considerations. a calorie count in every house.
a Before-&-After in every node. the Symphony of voyage is the only True Music.
Passage: what parallels polyphonic. enter Intersection Choreography, made
out of chaos. molecule jam Mumbojumbo. Friction is never not Fucking
or concomitance of closeness. to Bend or not to Bend all Somethings
in the air. I have been celestial before, I will be celestial again. I have returned from the
Demonstrative Retrograde by the parameters of meteorite, damiana
& quartz. organs of Untuned Torment, ring atmosphere hymns in Holiest
Chambers. Sing raspberry leaf. Sing Jupiter. the Surface of every illumination
expanding to consume its own Brilliance. a Detriment to the Witness
only. Go tell it! The answer is messenger Dead before delivery. Platonic
freefall through the center of the planet. On the Otherside a Low-Fidelity
Cartoon Reality still somehow better than this one & I've escaped
in the strongest-brewed-slop left within me. debris Deconstructed,
polished into magnanimity. Rejoice! the Hysteric & Mitochondrial.

Armatura

Pearls on a pitbull. Beast
in a ball gown. Ghost in
good shoes. Evergreen
eyeliner. Mountain beauty
mark. Monster of mascara
& might. Machine modify.
Make me over—obtuse
& opulent. Flowers on the flagrant.
Sex on the surveilled. Nightmare
in a negligee. Never a need, ever
an any-time tender. Lip-line
liar. Sleek sin slink. Wonder-
full of waste. Disaster in
decadence. Far gone-gilded.

_______ Makes Local Woman Cum

A. *visibility*

B. *representation*

C. *being kissed on the back of the neck*

[†]i'm ashamed. i claim to be patient
with my favorite donors. i know they want more.
sometimes less. my students know how i fumble
through the virtual space. i am covered
by my family, here & elsewhere but i'm trying
to imagine what adoring me would look like.
i put bundles in my kids' hands as a minor legacy.
they still seem to text when i need them most.
all my other loves have canceled their subscriptions.
remember who sees you.
remember how much of your humanity they hold.
remember who still wants you needy.

[‡]i'm easy. i claim to be excessive to my biggest fans.
i know they want more. my students write me emails to ask
why i look sad in the virtual space. i am embarrassed
for my friends & the pillars they are shackled to
but i'm waiting for food to be delivered.
i put a mushroom in a sandwich as a white flag
from my drag mother. all my kids seem to text
when i need them most. everyone i talk about
feels their ears burn.
remember who sees you
remember who hurts you. remember who demands
your forgiveness. remember who still wants you dead.

Show Me on The Doll Where America Is Better

i'm the doll. still living somehow.
i rent a room in a stolen dollhouse. on stolen land.
in an anarchistic jurisdiction. they lifted the ban
on teargas. just as the Proud Boys show up to fight
in solidarity with the capital circus coup.
theft of elections began with the electoral college.
the defense budget doesn't protect politicians
        so the fuck you thought bout us?
pigs roll over when lone wolf packs play paramilitary.
what happens when they grow feral & turn loose.
chocolate city is souring with spilled milk & nation-state.
sickness spreads from the source. sell a death song
featuring your favorite Black Woman Representative.
the ballot box is just another show of hands grasping
at power that don't belong to them & never did.
& they want it. the power. the doll. but they don't want
it to be better, just theirs.

Beginner's Astrology for Anarchist Jurisdictions in a Pandemic

They are a nation without sense, there is no discernment in them.

—Deuteronomy 32:28

From my driveway in North, I see at least three
drones each night. I have to count them.
Military aircraft change shifts around moon cycles.
There have been riots blocks away.
The Mayor of Portland bans teargas after bombing
a neighborhood. Sheriffs & state officers refuse to help local police.
local police take over the war crimes.
The smoke has cleared for now & we can see stars again.
I tattooed myself with The Star on my thigh. Upgraded my mask.
Is it grief, again? A shade of its own gift. This tender hit different.
The night says come hither, but the block stays viral.
I miss the streets but the armed & unmarked maneuver
malicious in plain sight. I understand the use of the North Star.
For a while, I could see her from my bed.

Before the Harvest Moon

I break a dozen eggs over my nephew's head & reserve a cabin in the woods by a creek for my family. I tell my daughter she's got more coming. The Office of the President cannot condemn white supremacy because the entire house is that shade. Obama convinced Black people we deserve to die here. We are unable to decipher the difference between saving & surviving. Yesterday, I was asked to be a mule. Today, a mother. Some matter. This cycle I'm choosing who receives. My people pop up on the map & I always know where my children are. Watching over like celestial like surveillance drone like becoming what haunts you & still data kills.

My nephew washes the egg off his face before learning about shame. I condemn the despair of Black children. I condemn the immobility to integrate imagination. My daughter points out my cravings spiking & the time of the month & I used to suffer in the mirror alone. I don't believe in the superstition. Nothing is born cursed. Cursed things curse beings. I don't create a practice of breaking mirrors but there never have been enough around for me to be so careless.

America's Love Language Is Evasion.

Telling my mommy I'm alive & not mad,
Telling my dad it's more complicated but to send money,
Telling my sister she's always known I've been this way,
Telling my children to carry less but be ready,
Telling my pup the leash is long enough,
Telling my night owl all the ways I want to sing,
Telling my demigod the donuts of my choosing,
Telling my dealer they are the true healthcare system,
Telling my housemate to get a new bed immediately,
Telling my internet wife we're in this dirty dish dystopia together
Telling the *Los Angeles Times* I'm gonna "try to be a hot bitch,"

PSA #18

we hereby declare now to be the end of end-of-days
we've been talking about apocalypse too long
    (don't daisies still sprout from the concrete?)
we guess we are still nuclear fatalities
    but none of this babble will be worth its breath in blood
    prophesy can't clean water or withstand radiation
we could argue we are doomed
    but we also believe that this is how things are to shake out
    (shake down? rot? play out?) we don't need truth
we have all read a version of the book of revelations
we all believe in our own gods
we have not concluded on the possible cowardice of rapture
we unanimously want this all to stop
we still recognize holidays
we spend dollars like they're different than trees
we don't need truth *(we don't need truth?)* we need good
we have an addiction to a succulent kind of convenience
    a rich & decadent desire to not deal we can't blame ourselves more than we already have
we don't need truth, we need prayers & thoughts
    we never wanted to be governed,we only wanted to sleep at night
we never wanted freedom,we only wanted rest
    best when it warms our hearts, but how combustible is our fragile hope
we want the worst of it to happen
we are constantly benefiting from the death of someone *else*.

Obligation #23 (TRANSPIRE)

all sniffling sneeze sense somatic cycle clinic-
al(l) strength system symptom of side-effected diss

order or cause all casual cold front coughing
congestion coagulates respite chronicle
respiration in spring sing seasonal season

hack up back of throat bloom caught act air cut careful
carry thick breathed lung leaves breaking through seam membrane
mucus memory mostly trapped airway passage

release exchange inhalation in exhaustion
eventual all exhausts & endurance ends
finality un-consequential conflation
fluctuates temperate terraforms or aspires

past not passed pressed or possessive in the present
spirit of supreme partiality be shift-
less lingering figure like ghost good haunt humor

hangéd man maybe upright woman wild card
deals no devil great no god life no limbo no-
body waits wonder bends will better beings want

Battleships in the Willamette

The internet says our river valley metropolis is overrun by a blue-haired, liberal bleeding farce who ignores the alleged rising of the crime rate. Our police stopped responding to nonviolent calls because they got mad when we kept firebombing their offices. Here, the mayor is the police chief.

When the fir trees were buried in snow, people died. When the cannabis farms were singed to ash, people died. The drones covered the night sky until the clouds stopped dissipating in late fall. Obscure aircraft of war did laps on clear spring afternoons in North just by the border. In early summertime, homes of local transients built outside my boyfriend's window only woke us up on wilder nights. Still, other citizens don't let them last two whole months. All the convenience store windows got busted, but the staff still calls me sweetheart or friend or darling…

The day after I first fuck my ex-girlfriend, we learn Roe v. Wade is overturned. My doctor approves my vasectomy inquiry in earnest. My pre-grown children pop around the city with more impunity than I can manage. Here, my hormones are free. My needles are not. My mind is on a waitlist. My blood panels come back unreactive. My boyfriend's surgery is mostly covered. The nurse mothers him like he's not him. The courthouse clerk calls me sir after filing my name & sex change. The courthouse clerk tells my son his dead name is so darn pretty. My landlord misgenders all my housemates. My neighbor says she knows I'm a woman because I'm so beautiful. My drivers usually call me brother & when they don't they seem to have a right to know what kind of wrong I am. Men still interrogate my hands at the checkout. I've only had to draw my lilac stun gun once on a white bundle of sticks outside the strip joint. My vaccines are available. My booster hurt the least. My tattoo artists are all hot. My esthetician is a trans girl. My nail tech is a goth queen. My crush plays a show at a club I can't go to anymore. Parties are superspreader events. Every so often, when outside, you can count the number of Black people on one hand. You'll see the matter of Black life posterized & paraded in car caravans or on the news in the Numbers.

In mid summertime, traffic is usually caused by spectators gawking at homeless encampment sweeps but today it is giant military ships towering between bridges along the river. Our city of overcooked carnation roses. Our city of semi-retractable bridges melting in the heat. They finally reopen cooling centers & offer free bus rides on the honor system. Relief from a natural disaster is a democratic city's optical illusion.
I make my healthcare a waterway.

Nine Twenty-Nine Twenty-Twenty

the last thing I read before bed
is the pandemic has one million kills
& I know better than to believe that number
& how am I to sleep? I ask, again
to all the evil tucked tight
in one thousand count thread sheets
& I want to burn down Jeff Bezos's estate
for not delivering the toilet paper overnight as I asked
& they say a million people died
because that's how many they can quantify
& the physiology of it all
remains a second-hand horror story. What if
there are no death songs in this nation's songbook?

Local Woman Is Not a Barbie

This Barbie cannot afford it.
Her dream house. The rent. The groceries.
She does not come with hand-me-downs.
She has an inheritance of plastic.
Her body is still fantastic & fickle.
This Barbie fell off the wagon.
With all her vice accessories.
She's not flexible, but her face is fixed.
Painted bare with stubborn shadows.
Her lips are something glossy.
Sometimes she glistens, sometimes she sweats.
This Barbie knows why Ken looks at her.
That way. Her imagination can be bent.
She wants not to be loved, she wants to be.
Wanted as an object before affection

Wanted as an object before affection.
She wants not to be loved, she wants to be.
That way her imagination can be bent.
This Barbie knows why Ken looks at her.
Sometimes she glistens, sometimes she sweats.
Her lips are something glossy.
Painted bare with stubborn shadows.
She's not flexible, but her face is fixed.
With all her vice accessories.
This Barbie fell off the wagon.
Her body is still fantastic & fickle

She has an inheritance of plastic.
She does not come with hand-me-downs.
Her dream house. The rent. The groceries.
This Barbie cannot afford it.

Why is *the doll* not aspirational?

Who Lived Happily Before This War?

And when they propagated kinder people's tweets, we

retweeted
but not enough, we quote-tweeted them but not

enough. tag me
in my #bed, around my bed Amerikkka

was typical: guilty house by guilty house by guilty house

I took a joint outside and sang to the moon

In the fourth year
of my hormones, in the land of terror

in the street of terror in the suburb of terror in the penthouse of terror
our blood country of terror, we can't forgive

who lived happily before this war.

Obligation #17 (TRANS LIFE)

we stay believing lies so i feel some type of way about teaching this lesson
learn a language that i can speak anywhere but home autobiographically
gibberish jumble junk function dysfunction retorts *y'all not gon listen so...*
i wanted to begin this with a lyric *fuck you* in the beginning Matter
made History by bribing The Now with The Yet To Be mark of recognizable self
dead names in Realtime Life's calling us mechanic copacetic aesthetics
a static staccato still tipping point politic play my whole hand's polemic
population of peril of people possible pleasure partitioned poses
posit a continuance continuum contained by catastrophe pulling
creation up to the cellular leveling labor lynched lightspeed libido
oral archives un-eldered untold telling tailspin tales spun from dust under tongues
somewhere where we can be seen & not heard about time we get something no roses
that's why i began so antagonistic i am allergic to most flowers
but mostly guilt the witness sickness alignment neutral chaotic curable
questions comradery costs so i keep keeping my own economic options
open ecology in obtuse outerlands margin magic majora makes
shapeshifter suspect spectral spectacle speaks easy enter here spatial haven
ether estuaries predating the words for body predicated elsewhere
there the empirical evidence suggests Everything has eventually
happened had been happening happy ending event ender this ain't about Death
i can talk about Life & representation all damn day but y'all covered that
poorly the pulse of The Movement is taken by a doctor who misgenders you
health care at-risk hearth carried cumbersome between communicable disaster
desire dissection the only autonomous act of practicality left
practitioners of the impalatable & all-encompassing patronage
pocket-sized prayer book of pliable particularities do play along
analogy of wiring or plumbing or revisionist's advanced placement

anyway we want so little more than wanting to want to want to want to want
to fuck to eat to sleep to cry to want to laugh to need to hate to want to want i want
to end this with a refrain, *fuck you fuck you fuck you fuck. you* fuck you get it right?

Obligation #15 (TRANSPOSE)

Habeas Corpus in
Corporal Habitat / Corporate
Herbivore
Coronated Heathen
Cornered Holy / ghoulish
in Form in Present or
Presentational Con / Convict
to Self-Inflict / Inflection flexible.

Show Me The Body Here
You Shall Have
The Body see *Habeas Corpus*
Or Here Show Me You Have
Seen Have My Body or Here
The Body Shall Have
Me or You Shall
Show All / You
Have
or The Body / Saw Me Showing
My Here

You Shall Have The Body
Have The Body You Shall
Shall You Have The Body?
The Body Shall Have You
The You Shall Have Body
The Body You Shall Have

Have You Had The Body?
She'll Have The Body Shell

Have The Body, Show Yours

Every Morning I Have to Make Sure This Is When I'm From

in this moment, i will take whatever design is available.
how many rituals done & undone, again? a humidity primed
for this spectacle. to say partial. how many times have i known
the other intimately? turn alarm into music. everyday,
some kind of orchestral moment. the nicer ways motionless,
molecular mobility maintains. create a pattern out of anything, movement
few things can claim forever even when bodies render themselves.
did i believe this way last time? next time, do i have to? acknowledge
let every lifeless thing i leave behind keep the element beneath my fluttering
is this better than another kind of faith? stomach a signal into a prayer—
a year. never was mine. each ending. end-time time bellowing forward.
lose the weather. not the atmosphere, yet same sky, another forecast. lost
i can't come back to tell myself: try something new. i believe i can.
today, it looks like mating season. calling the dance how i see it.

today, it looks like mating season. calling the dance how i see it.
i can't come back to tell myself: try something new. i believe i can
lose the weather, not the atmosphere, yet same sky, another forecast. lost.
a year never was mine. each ending. end-time time bellowing forward.
is this better than another kind of faith? stomach a signal into a prayer—
let every lifeless thing i leave behind keep the element beneath my fluttering
did i believe this way last time? next time, do i have to acknowledge?
few things can claim forever even when bodies render themselves
molecular mobility maintains. create a pattern out of anything: movement–
some kind of orchestral moment. the nicer ways motionless,
the other intimate? turn alarm into music, everyday.
for this spectacle to say partial. how many times have i known?

how many rituals done & undone, again? a humidity primed
in this moment, i will take whatever design is available.

La Belle Dame sans Merci

Vraiment, I'm down to fuck on the first date,
a Venusian detriment. Hostility is foreplay.

The etymology of mercy (from mercedem)
can mean a divine reward or vulgar pity.

I believe wanting to touch me deserves
a prize. I'm your trophy in a trapdoor.

The etymology of dame (from domina)
Can mean womanhood at home. So as a mother

I'm to act without wages. We know the wrong
ontologies of beauty. The Beholders, The Beheaded

at The Behest, The Best of Beyond. The Lack
of Complaint. I will sloppy swallow your soul

in thirty minutes or less & forget to charge
because greediness spoils my throat.

I'm easier than people seem to realize
but my unapproachability is a ministry

of defense. My fatale self is the most beautiful
girl I know. My basic instinct is a threat
a spectacular annihilation. Being is relentless

& my body needs sweat to activate its archive.

Signal the end of savior strategies. Only I can decide
to sacrifice my pussy & we have still too many licks

before us.

The Carpool Divorce Doll's Haibun

For Mason Hammer

Growing up in traffic, I would frequently spot people scamming the carpool lane with fictional structures appearing as corporeal occupants. Rarely a definitively faster way, the absurdity of the *carpool dolls*: e.g. a child seat filled with flour bags or literal life-size mannequins scantily clad. I never learned to drive so I'm a constant shortcut into the fast lane.

It's been 17 years since a man used me as an expressway. Like many others, my last lover was partnered. He tells me they're open so I get a side-piece without a secret. By our second date, his wife asked for divorce & he didn't realize he wouldn't need me anymore. All the utility of hanging by the door ends once you've been asked to leave the house.

In the passenger seat
The Doll combusts
Her arrival, his way out.

Accouterments

For JP

On the 400th birthday of America, my Un-boyfriend gave me a ring.
He wore a matching one & his best friend witnessed the transaction.
When we moved in together, he only helped me move my bedframe.
The one time he *really* touched me was in the wee hours of a new year,

slipping a $20 into my lace bralette. I made him retrieve it
& then he held me on the couch, in silence. We hugged every morning

with the coffee & lunch I provided. We hugged each night before bed
after last cigarettes. He never seemed to know when I went to sleep angry.

My collection is filled with reliable performances: apathetic to dependent.
I bought him shoes. His favorite candy. Dinner for months. He told me

all the ways he almost died & I fictioned his sainthood. A bird atop decrepit cathedral.
I used to wait for his bell to toll. He still lives in my dreams. Some of my mornings

still, ache for him & on better days I stay away from chaos. On weaker dawns,
I moan his name, hoping across town his ribs stiffen for a brief moment.

Orifice Jones

For JP

Today I am wearing my mother's wedding ring.
I stopped wearing the one my Un-boyfriend gave me because it was only a gift

& I needed to treat it as such. Ornament jams my frequency.
All my jewelry gotta be caught from somewhere. The esophagus is a pipe.

A faucet is present. Drip Season. Hard to lie with everything hanging out.
Any depth is hidden but access is unending. Organic jives

oscillating in more average levels every day. I'm telling everyone I know
about what's coming in. I am presently more development than research.

Past trials include: The Study of Fissure Maintained. A brief dance
around waste, blood, fear, inspection. The Study of Old Wound Memory.

The practicality of a scar, a tombstone, grown over. My fragility begins
with stories of tearing. Same riot-birth of near dismemberment. Then mouth

to feed, to teach. I learned no one knows the difference between
closeness and ephemera. I only pass as not passing. Today

I had more smoke than food. I am still getting used to loving this thing.
I am asking *are you well?* & mean it as an obvious joke.

Effie White Sings "Cellophane"

After FKA Twigs & Jennifer Hudson in Dreamgirls *(2007)*

Love me! It's just I haven't been feeling that well & hoping,
You was gonna love me! What about what's best for me?

They want to see us. The feelings that we had. They're waiting.
They're watching us. No, no, no, no way I'm living

Without you. All wrapped in cellophane & you
Want to see us apart? What about how I feel?

You're gonna love me & I don't want to have to share
Our love. I'm not living without you. I am telling you.

They want to see us alone. Why don't I do it?
For you. I'm not going. Didn't I do it for you?

You're the best I'll ever know. That's a lie! What about me?
I try: *I'm not enough*. I'm staying. They want to see us.

They're watching & I don't wanna be free.
There's no way I can ever go, just want to feel you're there.

They're hating, when all I do is for you? That's a lie!
What about what I need? When you're gone,

No, no, there's no way. I have no one to tell. But I get overwhelmed.
What about me? Why won't you do it for me?

unlucky duplex (slick mouth)[1]

after Sean Des Vignes & Jericho Brown

before my mouth deads this slick body.
   Sing. wax on testify come, honey come, O
they'd be honeycomb wax testimony song.
   later, stories better tell could tongue my If
tongue for a better story later.
   unbroken prepare, myself into fold I
fold into themselves prepared for breaking.
   gag, readies: grace by un-weaponed nails My
His hands grace a weapon ready to gag.
   .trouble of kind new a with eager become fingers His
what they are eager to finger & trouble.
   —done have hands my what him tell I &
He asks about what my hands do
.body my for slick too be mouth My

---

1. To be read from bottom to top, R-L then L-R, like a staircase.

Obligation #25 (TRANSACTION)

I CROSS MY LEGS I BRUSH
MY CLAVICLE / I PITCH MY
LAUGH I LAUGH I LOOK
AWAY / I SMILE I LOCK MY
WEIGHT IN MY RIGHT

HIP I POP TONGUE I SMEAR LIP
GLOSS I SLIP / ON HEELS I EAT WHEN I
CAN I AM NOT / ALWAYS FIXED I AM
TRYING ALWAYS NEW

MOVEMENTS I MOVE TO A
CITY THAT SWELLS / IN A RIVER
VALLEY I STILL SEE CROWS / I LOVED
A MAN WHO WAS MADE OF MORE

WANT THAN RELIABILITY
I LOVE / HIM I UNDRESS MYSELF
FOR WEATHERS / WILDING THEIR
WAY THROUGH THE TREES I PULL

CARDS NOW TOO I CAN SEE THERE
FROM HERE DO / I MENTION ECONOMY
AT THIS POINT / I COST I WANT & IT COSTS
TO WANT THIS.

Queen Frame

I make myself fit
into bags, luggage &
bed frames. my figure
folds into all wifely
positions. me, my own
damned spot. wed
to tragedy. my head
is known to make men
want blood. I have so much
spring in my structure.

Local Woman Believes There Is an Order to Our Days

To Maeve

I will fall in love with a barista, a bartender, and a corner store cashier. My myopic concerns conjecture minute missed connections. Some wet war of wild wander. *Some people choose to see the ugliness, the disarray.* What if this could be the forever I first designed to excavate? How long have I wanted to live in a town small enough to feel relevant? I try to blend into this new world. But here, in the river valley, my sentience becomes an evasive species. My mouth makes lesser predators nervous. Everywhere I go I begin to haunt it. A stop-traffic-double-take problem. Just today a man told me his first love & I share a name. I frequent places where I find handsome people. I want environments that host my particular beauty. I see how window becomes mirror as the sun moves into slow slumber.

To Delores

Our apex of the earth reaches a new year & I forget how I've been.
I've managed two good birthdays. The first was full of caution
but still so generous. My base frustrations with the city begin with me
& end in the silence I get for being alive & outside. All my crushes
look for lovers so far away. I miss how many no-string strangers opened me
before I chose this season of domesticity. I still want so much for my body.
I need to want so much more for my body. I remain in a square mile
of mind's brutality. My softness is a business that I manage in the red.
I am destabilized by the debt I owe for being. I wish I knew
something more than my cost. I triangulate my value from a market of proximity.
The closer you are the easier I am. I constantly raise my rates to leave the house
since the pandemic began. The first time I tried to work for cheap I collapsed.
Like a lone fir in a cemetery. *I choose to see the beauty.*

A Man I [____] Is Bartending

For Sean

We talk about gore & erotic thrillers.
A lonely woman interjects regularly.
The night is slow. I get to have some of him to myself.
We had plans, he & I. Tonight, he has to work
so I came to see him. He never makes me pay.
He just gives. He's decidedly unaffectionate
but he hugs me. His eyes are a lake in the desert.
I hold my breath when he smiles at me.
He doesn't usually bartend. He cooks.
He usually feeds me. But tonight, it's all liquid.
I watch him play nice. He's affable when needed.
I dream of being what he needs. Tonight I'm just company.
He looks at me after every quip with a customer.
I have to laugh. He sings along with what's playing overhead.
I harmonize under my breath. The soundtrack is 80's new wave.
He reminds me of his age & I tell him I like wisdom.
We were supposed to be elsewhere tonight,
but he's here, so I'm here with him.
He never tells me everything but I know
when something is wrong. I wish he used me more
but I love how little he asks when he gives so much.

Local Woman Goes Home with Men

who can't finish. They need her attention
as much as she wants theirs. In the wee hours,

men try to hold everything together. They politic poorly
& drum in basements & play A Tribe Called Quest.

They've at least bought her drinks. At least.
She's generous or easy depending on the attack angle.

Few keep her till dawn. Most men combust. Fumble her
frequently. They slip & remind her how minuscule

men can be. She towers, but her girlfriends tell her
she crumbles at the foulest gaze. She was adored as a child

& now she's a spoiled thing. She rots anytime she feels
less than a woman. Men remind her she is a void.

My Ex-Fiancé Calls Me Darling

For WTM

So I tattoo it on my gut. He wears Sir on his spine.
I call him that to remind him his body costs

Both of us. Ink the way we fit
in each other's mouths.

He tells me he'd be my wingman
& I'm envious he lives in a world without jealousy.

Me, a lustful & seething thing. Only satiated
by a narcissistic temperament. I wanted him

To have my name on his throat,
but he has other lovers who kiss there.

I never feel like the chosen one, but I believe
myself a gift. How precious can I be?

I'm passed & placed & pedestaled unable
to satisfy. I'm an excellent excuse to resist.

We replace names with titles & remind each other
of all the texts we share. I am allowed

To feel pain in his hands. I kiss the bandage
while he dreams. I tell him my history

Of infidelity. He doesn't care. I tell him
I am only approached by men who like

but never need. He doesn't hear how I fear
he fits the bill. If the intensity we harmonize

is just a song, not a symphony. Do I vocalize
the instruments that aren't there? Before I leave

his bed, I want to hurt less. I want him to miss me,
he licks my gut & thanks me for my response.

Every Father I See Is My Ex-Fiancé

For WTM

Every mother is me,
unless she's dressed frumpy.
I swear to my man

I'll never dress boring.
My children will not make me
ugly. My hips have widened

& my ass is bigger. Transitive properties
of distribution. I want us to afford a family.
My ex-girlfriend tells me

she doesn't wanna have a kid poor.
My mother had me in the middle class
but raised me in the projects

with two Masters. She tells me the ghetto
is not where you are but how you feel.
I feel like raising my children on Jupiter.

My ex-fiancé tells me
we've known each other for 800 years
& I believe him.

How many children have we propagated
since the 13th century? I hope to have been
a better mother before now. I hope to be

a better mother again. Every little boy
with long hair is mine. Every little girl
with colored hair is mine. Every child

with obtuse hair is mine. I dream
of every Black child's smile. I cover
every trans kid's glee in glitter.

My womb is a nuclear reactor
& my offspring are the latest technology.
all prototypically possible.

Daddy Feeding

For Jimmy, Beto, & Joel

Every time I see
the daddy next door
he feeds me.
cherries, grapes,
artisanal pastries
with chocolate cream
& mixed berries.
He feeds me
with his hands
dangling sweets
over my mouth
watching
my lips take
the shape
of each delight.

The difference between a man & daddy is who feeds me.
I never have to lift a finger for daddy.

He puts sparkling water
by my bedside
before I come
over.
He gets me
an extra blanket
before I have to ask.

Every time I see
the daddy from the bar
he gives me
something.
Fresh Blunt,
Free Drink,
$1000
just for being pretty.
One time
he had me
order him food
because he was
too exhausted.
He was sad
when I didn't
get anything
for myself.
The last time
I saw him
he picked me up
from my house
just to drive around.
He asks
to feed me
nachos
& I salivate.
He pays
for everything.

I eat money
so currency
is a sinister kind
of nourishment.
I never have to
sustain myself
with a daddy.
They take care
of the needs
they want.

Every daddy wants me
to love their daughters.
Every daddy suckles
my titties like sons.

I dream of stepmotherhood.

The difference between a man & daddy is knowing I want to be a mother. They imagine me as both hole & hearth. Vessel & vehicle. Worry & womb.

Every Daddy wants to do more for me. They want me paid, fucked & satisfied. They want me filled in their presence. This is how I know they see me as a woman. They want me cared for. They want me full.

Presently, I Only Want to Understand Being Full & Fed

My roommate reminds me to notice the moon. I think of its regularity & mine. The moon can't make me feel *better*. Though the whole sky keeps wild folk wild. Hysteric. My throat gets swollen-but-not-sore & I lipsync my favorite Whitney songs to exercise The Muscles. Making out is my favorite cure. But when I can't, I fuck more aggressively & get more compliments & free electrical rewiring. I want to stop smoking & I need to keep fucking. I'll pay for a manicure before food. Keep a roof over my head by the Grace of the universe. I get hungry & feed myself on existential poetry & romantic ideas of labor. My horoscope can't be found in a magazine. I look to the stars for their music. I decide to allow the radiation to vibrate my bones & I'm still fucking to be touched. Learning how to be flexible & exhale. *I have been celestial before & I will be celestial again*. I'm back from an exile with new tools for magic. Attempting to purify my body with artisanal herbal blends & Youtube videos of space sounds. I think highly of my attempts toward improvement which I'm learning can annoy everyone I love. I take so many things too seriously, spiral into parallel understandings: impossible & still better. Somehow I've made it to the other side of here with most of my best parts intact.

Cradle for The Doll, Coffin for The Boy

To Narcissus

All my toys were knives
& pills & leather, or acrylic.

I infantilized the performance
of gestation toward manhood.

The water line is the distance
between legal maturation & the beginning of my reign.

I don't want to be queen
but live unquestionably as a ruler.

My first act as an entity was eulogizing
the every-other-timeline branches.

The Boy's coffin disintegrates into the bubbling delta.
Daffodils bloom at the apex of grave & marsh.

I cut a full blossom & tie it to my wrist.
She sees the fatal refraction of her soldered self

with forgiveness. Echo cries. Nemesis appears differently
in future myths. From the beginning, when I imagined life

off the shelf, I thought to market my body
a lavender dreamhouse.

The Boy disintegrates into the river.
There is no wilderness heavy enough to contain me.

A tributary is a warpath. The Boy on a suicide mission.
& I, a relentless sweetheart.

The river's refraction works only as memorabilia.
I require intentional positioning & regular maintenance.

Local Woman Obliges (TRANSSEXUAL)

I want to be all the things I promised
myself. Finding a way to be nearby,
to be neighborly & to be known.

Every day I decide to believe
in my own face. My devotion keeps me
close & edging. I am put under oath
declaring my growing territories
bound to a body, a place & a time.

All of my wants whistle out the window.
What are morals to the demoralized?

What word of my mine can you take? What is near?
Not always what feels close but what holds tight?

Commitment calls for keeping a distance.
My bits are better when you're indebted.
I swallow necessity each morning.

What Is the Bottom

Of a woman? An ocean floor. The meniscus line on a syringe.
Interiors can be entered from other places than the rear.

My personal history with penetration includes guzzled throat
songs & a predilection for ink. Or *alls my life* I was a top, until

I became a woman, then I was a tool. Now I reclaim myself:
a vessel. In my mid-heaven Cancer rules, wet & claws out.

The week before I started injecting estradiol intramuscularly,
I began letting a man inside me for the first time in a half-decade.

My personal history with penetration includes mediocre care
& lingering violence. Or *ain't nobody* knocked on the right door.

But, welcome to this newly open house overlooking the water.
She's quite the estate & there's a party in the back.

Acknowledgments

Elderly Mag: "Local Woman Raises Lazarus," "Local Woman Acts Much Too Alone in Her Body, Yet Lonely No More," "America's Love Language Is Evasion"

Georgia Review: "Beginner's Astrology for Anarchist Jurisdictions in a Pandemic," "Nine Twenty-Nine Twenty-Twenty"

Poetry Magazine: "Orifice Jones"

Bennington Review: "unlucky duplex (slick mouth)," "Every Morning I Have to Make Sure This Is When I'm From"

Protean Mag: "Who Lived Happily Before This War?"

PANGYRUS: "Before the Harvest Moon"

Baest Journal: "Presently, I Only Want to Understand Being Full & Feeding"

THNX:

giving glory & honor to every woman, locally & globally for providing a framework for me to see myself through.

to Mommy, you continually teach me how grown i can be.
to Siaara, you've loved local since she was just a reflection in a stream.
to Candace, you just {redacted} so i feel safe inside you.
to Erika, Ahya, Fatima, Aaryn, Natasha, Simone, Rlynn; your sisterhood molded me.
to the numerous dolls, dykes, comrades, divas, hookers, teachers, & philosophers
who located me in womanhood, y'all ate that & yet i'm fed.

to Presentt, LV, Chri'shawn, Mona, Cody, Masyn, Trouble: because of y'all, i mother.

to Bare Bones, Belmont Inn, The Vern, Babydoll Pizza, Taqueria Los Punales, Nail Church, Hollywood Vintage, & all the establishments in Portland that have set the scene for this collection: stay weird!

to my knights, Brandon, Derrick, Cal, Gregory, Jack, Andy, Big Sean, Lance, Joseph, Steffan, & my dearest Aeon Famous– i feel safer with you all surrounding me.

to the other men: you all owe me apologies & still i'm sorry.

Jzl Jmz (pronounced juh-zell jaym-s) aka [Lady Tournament] is a Black Los Angelena and award-winning Transsexual based in Portland, OR. Her early professional career included positions at *The Huffington Post* and *The Offing*. Her work has been featured in the *Los Angeles Times*, *Poetry Magazine*, *Oprah Magazine*, *Ms. Magazine*, *PEN America*, *Willamette Weekly*, and several anthologies. She's the author of three full-length poetry collections: *Mannish Tongues* (2017); *The Black Condition ft. Narcissus* (2019), which received the Poetry Center Book Award; and *Local Woman* (2025). Her film and performance work has been taught and toured nationwide. She has been a Lambda Literary Fellow and a Precipice Art Grant Recipient through Portland's Institute of Contemporary Art. Her first sculpture exhibition ROOMinnate was shown at the Ori Gallery in 2024. She's an occasional rapper, founder of Tournament Haus Mutual Aid Fund, and co-founder of FamousFestPDX.

NIGHTBOAT BOOKS

Nightboat Books, a nonprofit organization, seeks to develop audiences for writers whose work resists convention and transcends boundaries. We publish books rich with poignancy, intelligence, and risk. Please visit nightboat.org to learn about our titles and how you can support our future publications.

The following individuals have supported the publication of this book. We thank them for their generosity and commitment to the mission of Nightboat Books:

Kazim Ali • Anonymous (4) • Ava Aviva Avnisan • Jean C. Ballantyne • Will Blythe • V. Shannon Clyne • Theodore Cornwell • Ulla Dydo Charitable Fund • Gisela Gamper • Photios Giovanis • Amanda Greenberger • David Groff • Parag Rajendra Khandhar • Katy Lederer • Shari Leinwand • Elizabeth Madans • Ricardo Maldonado • Ethan Mitchell • Caren Motika • Elizabeth Motika • Asker Saeed • The Leslie Scalapino - O Books Fund • Amy Scholder • Thomas Shardlow • Benjamin Taylor • Jerrie Whitfield & Richard Motika • Clay Williams

This book is made possible, in part, by grants from the National Endowment for the Arts, New York City Department of Cultural Affairs in partnership with the City Council, and the New York State Council on the Arts Literature Program.

NATIONAL ENDOWMENT for the ARTS arts.gov · NYC Cultural Affairs · NEW YORK STATE OF OPPORTUNITY. Council on the Arts